The Psychic Time Traveler

The Psychic Time Traveler

How You Can Change Your Past and You're Future

WE ALL CAN DO IT!!

• • •

Tim D Beaton

ISBN-13: 9780998719207
ISBN-10: 099871920X

June 19, 2014

I WAS BORN IN ALASKA in 1963. My grandfather was John Beaton, the man who discovered the great Iditarod Gold fields on Christmas Day of 1908. My dad, Neil Sr., had a gold claim north of the Yukon and had done construction and gold mining along with firefighting and commercial fishing most of his life. He was a pilot and an air navigator in World War II.

Following in the footsteps of these great men, I have always felt that I had some kind of special abilities. I first noticed something was up when I was thirteen years old. My mother was sleeping in the living room, and I was in my bedroom. I closed my eyes, and I thought, "Mom, come quick! Help me! Help me!"

Within ten seconds, she busted in the room and asked, "What's going on? Are you OK?" I had not said a word. I had just been thinking it. I told her that I was OK and that she must have been dreaming.

1979

When I was sixteen years old, we were living in Seattle. I was on the phone with my first girlfriend, Heather, until about two o'clock in the morning. I was in love—puppy love, but still love. After our conversation, I was ready for bed, exhausted from the day's activity. It was a hot summer night. I remember it was too hot to wear clothes or even covers. I fell asleep fast. When I woke up, I was two inches from the ceiling. I looked around, and I could see myself lying in my bed. It was the most peaceful and tranquil feeling that I have ever felt. I thought to myself, "I must be dead." I didn't want to die just yet. Thinking of my girlfriend, Heather, I managed to get back into my body.

I woke up dripping cold sweat and saying to myself, "Never do that again. Never do that again!"

For several days, I did not tell anyone about my experience. Angela, a wise old lady, came over to visit with my mother. I told her what happened. She explained to me that I had an *out-of-body experience*. I later learned it was also called *astral projection*. I have tried to duplicate it many times since then; however, I've had no success. Still, every once in a while, I try to recreate the experience. What an amazing feeling, and knowing what I know now, I would have no trouble traveling through space-time.

1991

Many years went by, and I was running a business repairing office equipment. I would often have to go out with my technicians to help them figure out a problem machine. On one occasion, I recall looking at the mirrors of a copier and thinking, "Wow! He didn't even clean the mirrors of the copier."

When I was about to mention that to him, he said, "No, Tim. I cleaned the mirrors. I know I did."

I looked at him and said, "I didn't say anything."

He said, "You said I didn't clean the mirrors."

That was what I had been thinking, but I had not said it. We both thought that was odd, and we went back to work.

When I needed extra money to pay bills or buy something important, I would get very stressed over it. By the next day, someone would come in and buy a copier, or I would receive a large check that would satisfy my needs. I felt that when I needed something, the universe would somehow present it in short order.

1992

I was struggling with some personal issues. I was very upset and so very angry with an ex-girlfriend. Shit happened. I was up all night, and in the morning, I was too upset and tired to go to work. I started drinking Bacardi. I asked my current girlfriend, Teresa, to handle things at the office on her own that day. I told her that I was not going to be able to work; I was too upset and too pissed off. I had two or three drinks and was ready to pass out. I had been up all night dealing with this problem. I finally fell into a restless sleep, colored with rage and anger, the likes of which I have never felt before. I started to dream:

I was in a field. There was an old-style well, the kind with a wheel and a rope. A bucket could come up with water in it. The rocks that made up the well we're very pores. They almost looked like lava rocks.

> In my dream, I was still full of rage. I wanted to summon a demon out of that well. I concentrated and concentrated until I heard scratching coming from inside the well. Without speaking a word, I was telling the demon what I wanted him to do. He understood me perfectly. All I needed to do for him was to get him out of the well. When he was almost at the top, I saw his hand reaching over the bricks of the well. He had three crablike claws on his hand. They were as big as the armrest of a chair. He began to edge out of the well.

The phone rang and woke me up. It was Teresa calling from my office. She pleaded with me to stop whatever I was doing immediately. Whatever I was doing was causing her to smell burning flesh, and she had a horrible taste in her mouth. She begged me multiple times to stop what I was doing "for God's sake!" I was still in a state of rage and wanted the demon to come out of the well. I explained the dream to her, and she told me that she felt it, and it scared her very badly. It scared her so much that she had called me at the moment the demon was almost out of its prison. It took me several hours to get back to sleep. I was able to find the field that I was in.

It was full of the same type of rocks that the well was made out of. But the well was no longer there I could not find the well again. At the time, I felt that the demon would have actually manifested into reality. It was so real. A short time after my dream the volcano Mount superior erupted blanketed Anchorage with 3 inches of ass. It was 1992.

A few years later, I dated a lady named Melinda. We hit it off pretty well. Several months into our relationship, she told me that she had seen me in a dream years before she met me. She was positive it had been me. After one year of dating, we moved in together, although I kept my own place.

Melinda ran an adult residential facility in Alaska. Her father had left her a trust fund, but she could not touch it until she was thirty-one. When she turned thirty-one, she decided to leave Alaska and move back to Louisiana. We were in love, or so we thought. I decided to go with her and sold my house.

We went to Louisiana and purchased an old house. We remodeled it and turned it into a duplex. Melinda's first husband was from Guatemala, and she had a lot of good friends there. We stayed in Louisiana for three years.

Eventually Melinda wanted to move back to Guatemala, so we packed up the car and drove through Mexico to Guatemala. We rented a house in the mountains for eighty dollars a month. There was a banana orchard in the backyard and a large avocado tree in the front yard. It had three bedrooms, and one of the rooms was a worship room. That room we turned into a bedroom because it needed the fewest repairs.

After settling in, we started running a small gold mine three miles from our house in a place called El Rancho. The year was 2000.

One morning, I dreamed that I cut my hand. I woke up screaming. I was holding my wrist, and as I was waking up, I could see my hand closing where I cut it. I explained the dream to Melinda, saying that I was back in Alaska, cleaning panes of glass with a razor blade. I was going to cut the glass and reframe some pictures that I had. I also explained that I had no plans at that time to go back to Anchorage. so that I had nothing to worry about. The year was 2001.

Several years later, Melinda and I broke up. I had to go back to Alaska to deal with some property that I had to liquidate. The person who was buying it from me wanted to cash out. The year was 2003.

After closing the deal, I purchased another home. I met a young lady named Mary. After we dated for several months, she moved in with me. Her mother, Judy, had a farm in Oregon. Judy's husband, Joe, was diagnosed with cancer, and Mary planned on moving back to the farm to help out with Joe's care. She loved Joe very much. I rented out my home, and we bought a van, packed it up, and headed out of Alaska in late January. We drove to Oregon, where I stayed for the winter.

I came back to Alaska to get ready for the gold-mining season. My sister had secured an investor who would help us buy a couple of dozers and some gear and equipment to fire up Dad's old gold claim. When Dad worked on it, he had been taking out one hundred ounces every ten days.

While still in Anchorage, I wanted to reframe some pictures that I had shipped from Guatemala. I removed the glass so the freight would not be so expensive. I was cleaning some glass with a razor blade, and I cut my hand, severing two tendons, my pinky, and my ring finger. I saw a one-inch gash in my hand, grabbed my wrist, and started screaming.

I remembered the dream right then, but that was not my main concern at that moment. I spent a week going to the hospital and getting my hands fixed up. I had to wear a cast for nine weeks and was heavily sedated for the pain. It was hard for me to take care of myself, so I went back to Oregon where Mary could take care of me. Thank you, Mary! Time went by, and I ended up staying with her for five years.

When I was in Oregon, I played the lottery, like everyone else does. One morning, I found myself having a dream about the lottery numbers. I argued with myself in the dream that the number was too big—there was no number 11,119 in the lottery. I argued with myself, but I could not get past this number. It was just too big. This number wasn't even a choice. I woke up, and it dawned on me that all the numbers were squished together. I remember all the numbers were on a black background, almost like a chalkboard. The numbers also appeared to be a hazy white. So I played the lottery, and lo and behold—the first numbers were 1, 11, and 19. After that, I kept a pen and paper close to my headboard in case I had the dream again. I constantly asked myself who would be sending me the lottery numbers. I thought of a divine influence such as Jesus or God. Other than that, I had no clue. I had one more dream close to that time frame as well, but I do not recall the outcome. I know I did not win the lottery. The year was 2005.

One more thing I remember—over the years, I have had a strange feeling of something coming out of my shoulder blades. I imagined that they were angel wings. But I could not determine if they were white or black—were they representing the good or the evil inside of me? I have not had those feelings in twenty years, so maybe they were just growing pains.

These are the odd things that have happened that have made me think that I have special abilities.

In 2007, I was out at the gold mine, and I called Mary to see how things were going. She informed me that she had new friends and that things would have to change when I got home. What that meant to me is that she had found herself a new boyfriend.

When I got home, I discovered that indeed was the case. Over the years, it seems I always lose my girlfriend when I come out to the gold mine for four months. I have a wall of photographs of lost loves.

In Mary's travels, she came across a movie that she wanted me to watch, called *What the Bleep!? Down the Rabbit Hole*. It was about quantum physics and string theory and a little bit about time travel. I have watched this show at least twenty times. This show helped define my ideas about time travel. If you are reading this book, I strongly suggest that you purchase that movie; it is definitely interesting and full of information.

I was lying in bed, depressed that I did not do the reality TV show about gold mining in Alaska. My sister had the idea three years before a show aired with those colorful characters, the Hoffman Family.

I was in bed, depressed, for three days. The first day it came to me out of the blue that I needed to win the lottery. But how? Then I remembered seeing the numbers and seeing my hand get cut years before it happened. I felt like someone was blowing into my face.

What if I could see into the future and see the winning numbers before they were drawn? That's all I would need to do. It sounded simple enough. I got chills through my whole body thinking about this. The second day I was still in bed, depressed, and it came to me in the same way. It was almost like someone was sending me a blueprint about how to set up a reality show on how I won the lottery using psychic time travel. The third day, October 10, 2013, was a very special day; something really wonderful, which could change the way people think, was also revealed to me. I will touch on that at the end of this book.

Since my vision, I have been trying to come up with different techniques to send myself the lottery numbers. I have purchased many items to help me with this, such as a menu board from Costco with lights that flash and change to different colors. I also purchased an old chalkboard from an estate sale. Apparently the chalkboard came out of an old school in Virginia, the state where I currently live. I also purchased a small roulette wheel. It is a good game to practice on.

After the winning numbers are drawn, I write them on the chalkboard and my menu board. I memorize them as I am looking at them, trying to send them back to myself in time. It seems that I only receive the numbers during a state of sleep. If I am awake and guess the numbers, I do very poorly. Sometime during the day, I will try to relax, close my eyes, and think of the numbers. I will write down twenty or thirty guesses on a piece of paper. I will not play the numbers, but I will watch to see if I was close. This saves a lot of money while I practice. I also try to receive the numbers in the morning just before I open my eyes. I am constantly thinking of new psychic time-travel techniques.

While I was in Virginia two months ago, I got up and saw several numbers: 2, 3, 9, 12, 27, and 35. I was quite excited because that was the first time that I had received numbers since I'd been practicing. I had just purchased the chalkboard and was using it. I played the lottery that day, and the winning numbers were 2, 3, 12, 27, 38, and 17. Looking back, I recall adding the 9 and 35 as I was waking up. I got four out of the six numbers, which only paid one hundred dollars. But I was happy to recoup some of the money that I had already spent on the lottery. I was very excited that I was able to send myself those numbers and that I was on the right path

My wife, who is a nonbeliever in my ability with time travel, said it was a lucky guess and that it's more intuition than anything else. She spoiled my moment of excitement, so I pondered what she said and thought about intuition.

What is intuition? The ability to understand something immediately without the need of conscious reasoning.

I pondered that for a while, and I tried to see if it would fit into my time-travel thoughts. I determined that intuition, déjà vu, premonition, precognition, and a gut feeling could all be forms of psychic time travel. We have just been calling it by different names. I feel that if we understand and believe that these feelings are messages to ourselves from the future, and if we are enlightened as to what these messages actually are, we will pay closer attention to them. This could change everybody's life for the better.

I perceive some of these precognitions as warnings. I recall sometimes having an ominous feeling as I get into my car, and then the next day, I would get a traffic ticket or get into a car accident. This has happened to me many times. Now when I get these feelings, I stay home until they pass, no matter what event I have planned. I feel that these are messages coming back to me from myself through psychic time travel, trying to warn me of future problems or disasters. When I am driving too fast, I get that feeling. I will slow down, thinking there might be a police officer up ahead, and in more than one instance, that was actually the case.

When I left Virginia to go to the gold mine in Alaska, I stopped in Oregon to visit with my ex-girlfriend Mary's mother, Judy. She adopted me after the breakup, and we have been close friends ever since. Judy's daughter Sue picked me up from the airport. On our ride back to Judy's house, I was explaining to Sue my time-travel theory. Going through the whole scenario about seeing the lottery numbers in a dream and wondering who would be sending those numbers to me, it dawned on me that I learn how to do it in the future and send them back to myself.

Sue   Tim   Judy

When I visit Judy, we always go to the casino on Thursday for the seafood buffet. While there, I like to play roulette using my new techniques and understanding of Space-time memory transfer.

I start with twenty dollars and ask for five-dollar chips. I use one chip and place it on one number. I also stand behind the glass where the roulette wheel is, without betting. I try to see the numbers before they land. This technique saves a lot of money on practicing.

Judy and I watched the roulette wheel from behind the glass. I turned to her and said, "Number one is going to hit next. Should I bet my hundred-dollar chip?"

She said, "Hell, no! That's too much!"

I agreed with her. I walked around to an open seat and asked for five-dollar chips, and I put one five-dollar chip on the number one. As the ball was rolling, I put another five-dollar chip on number one and told the gentleman running the game that number one was a sure bet. Everyone around us had overheard my conversation with Judy that number one was going to hit. It did! The gentleman running the roulette table looked a little surprised. I had won $360. Judy suggested that we cash out. I handed Judy the large stacks of five-dollar chips and asked her to go cash them in for me. I played another sixty dollars with no success. Thanks to Judy's persistence in encouraging me to take the money and run, I did not go home broke that night.

2015

On another occasion, I went to the coast with a friend of mine named Ruby to see a concert at a different casino. I told her about my newfound ideas and that she was going to be impressed with me at the roulette table. I was just being cocky at the time, so I bought twenty dollars' worth of five-dollar chips. I bet on the number six; I won. I bet on the number four; I won. I bet on the number eight, and I won! The next number I thought of was thirty-six, but I would have had to reach over two people to place it on thirty-six. So I settled on seventeen, but of course thirty-six hit. Frustrated with myself, I gathered up my $900, and we left.

On our ride home, I explained to her my thoughts on time travel. I was telling her about seeing the lottery numbers in my dream.

Somewhere in the future, I learned how to send the numbers back to myself to try to change my past. Yet I think, "If I had won the lottery back then, it would be highly unlikely that I would have ever followed this time-travel path that I am on now. Therefore, Tim, in the past, would never have learned time travel and would have never sent the message back to me." Kind of confusing, isn't it?

Ruby had a story of her own to tell. Her mother had a dream about the lottery numbers. She went and played them and won $70,000. So it was not hard to convince Ruby of my new vision.

In *What the Bleep!? Down the Rabbit Hole*, which I mentioned earlier, every one of those events can be explained through quantum mechanics, even the manifestation of the demon. Apparently, every one of us has this ability. I am hoping to enlighten as many people as possible to their true potential. I want them to realize the endless possibilities for their future and a way to change their past.

June 22, 2014

To explain this next paragraph keep in mind the name of the book was going to be, how I won the lottery Using Time Travel.

I had not won the lottery as of that point. Are you surprised that I am writing a book about winning the lottery using time travel to see into the future and recover the numbers? Well, if I do not win, you will probably never get to read this book, and you really need to read this book. So I'm saying that I still have to win—for you.

My plan was to win the lottery and do a weekly reality show on how I won it, how I was going to invest the money I won, and how I was going to change my life (and hopefully change yours) by showing you how I did it, letting you know you can do it too. The techniques are simple. You have to be aware of what you're doing. If you feel something whispering in the dark recesses of your mind, pay close attention. Have the understanding that it could be you sending yourself a message back in time to tell you about upcoming lottery numbers, problems, or disasters.

I'm sure we all have a story or two to share. Since I have been talking with different people and telling them about my new time-travel concept, I have been hearing a lot of good stories about their own experience of seeing into the future. I have a good friend named Tammy whom I discussed this with early on. She told me of a dream she had when she was eleven. She dreamed that her mother was in an airplane crash. Her mother was leaving to go visit friends in another state. She told her mother about the dream. Her mother assured her it would be all right, and she would be OK. Her mother made it to her friends safe and sound. Three days later, when she was coming home, the plane crashed; there were no survivors. It was a very sad experience for her.

I asked her if she thought she had seen into the future. She said she wasn't sure, but she saw the plane crash before it happened. She never called it time travel; she called it something else. I wonder if she would have known at the time to call it Space-time memory transfer.

if it would have made a difference in saving her mother and all the other people on the planet. And were there any other people who had that same dream about a loved one? We talked at length about time travel and what the current understanding of time travel is. The current understanding of time travel is that a human is transported from one time to another and physically stands in a different time. That's what we have determined that time travel means for the general populace.

Tammy said we should call it mind travel because I was not physically transporting myself to a different time but using my mind to go to a different time or send messages back to myself.

That is how we came up with the phrase "mind travel." Thank you, Tammy.

(October 20, 2013)

ON JANUARY 17, 2017

I have come up with different phrases that may fit better. Psychic time travel, space-time memory transfer, Self-preservation premonition space time memory transfer—which one do you like best?

Once, I was at my mining camp in Alaska. There was a noise at the door. At first, I thought, "Oh boy! I have a visitor." I quickly remembered that I was out there by myself. It turned out to be a black bear. I looked out of my side window for a few minutes, and it finally appeared. I banged on my window, and it ran about ten yards from my building. I opened the door and fired my shotgun over its head, hoping to scare it away. It seemed to work. I hoped it would not come back. I would try to scare it off next time, but if it kept coming back, I would have to put it down. Our cookhouse out there had been broken into and totally destroyed two times. I did not think it was this bear. It was too small. It must have been passing through looking for a good fishing hole.

June 23, 2014, 1:50 p.m.

The bear came back one morning at 9:00 a.m. I got dressed and went outside to see if I could pepper spray it to scare it off. By the time I got dressed, it was already gone. I wonder if it got a feeling there was trouble coming and ran off.

So how do I get back into my time-travel story from this interruption?

I was talking earlier about people I have spoken with about my time-travel theory. I decided to place an ad to see if I could find some other stories in which people had a dream before something incredible happened.

June 23, 2014

I placed an ad on Craigslist, and believe it or not, I got a few interesting stories. Here are my ad and their stories,

> Hello. My name is Tim. I am writing a book, and I need your help. I am looking for people who have had déjà vu or dreams/nightmares that came true. If you can write a quick story about your dream or déjà vu, I would appreciate it. For example, a friend of mine, when she was eleven, dreamed of a plane crashing with her mother on it. One week later, her mother's plane crashed. I hope your story has a happier ending, but if not, I would still love to hear it. Please put "déjà vu" in the title so I can weed out your story from all of the spam that I get. Thanks!

> **Kasey**
> I have been getting them for as long as I can remember (I'm sixty-two). Some of them happened years before they came to be, others only a few days or weeks. I had a recurring one that started when I was a child. I had dreamed it many times until it came true. I was in a dentist's chair in my twenties. I knew I had been there before because I knew exactly what the dentist and his assistant were going to say. It went on for about five minutes, and I never had the dream again.

Tim's Comments
So in this psychic time-travel experience, what if you had yelled out "Buy Apple stocks!"? Or what if you yelled out contacted Tim's time zone in 2001 and tell them that the twin towers were going to be taken down by 747s on 9/11? Think of the possibilities to change your past. What message could you send yourself back in time? Each one of us has one special message.

Kasey
I forgot to mention that I have had dreams of correct lotto numbers twice; unfortunately, I didn't realize that they were lotto numbers. I only realized it when I saw the numbers, once on TV and once in the paper, just like in the dreams.

Tim's Comments
I also have had dreams of the lottery numbers. Sending lottery numbers back to ourselves might be common. What would your first wish be if you rubbed the magic lantern? To be wealthy?

Speed Racer
Hey,
I had a dream around May 31 or June 1 about my car freezing up while I was driving, and it was hard to turn. The car broke down, and in my dream, I was stuck. I've never had problems with it before, and I take care of it. It's a nice sports car. The next day, I drove it, and I downshifted and had some fun. Next thing I know, the engine goes clunk, steering wheel freezes up, and I have to muscle the wheel in order for it to turn. Turns out, the alternator belts crapped out on me. I just had that dream and then this. I

love my car and had it for three years. This was insane. I've had dreams come true before, but this was crazy because it was the dream to a T. Maybe when people have a deep connection with something they care about, they see things ahead, even if it is a car.

Bonnie

Hi. Being curious, I looked under the heading on Craigslist entitled "Rants and Raves" because of a bad experience with Radio Shack. I came across your ad. What you are searching for is who I am; I am clairvoyant and can offer you the experiences of my life, as I was born with this amazing gift and am able to time travel. My name is Bonnie, and I am a very unique person, as I live my life with the experiences you are researching. This is more than just déjà vu; if this is too much for your writing, I understand. Even in this day and age, it is difficult to find people like me, so it's even harder for people to accept. I would like to share this knowledge that I have. My e-mail address is as follows…

Ken

Hi. I read your post in the "R and R" section, and I have had dreams that have come true before, but it'll take me a few to remember some of them. Some are military related, and some are civilian related, but one I do remember off-hand. I had a dream that I was driving down a road on my way to work, not wearing my seat belt, and I died in a car crash. The next morning, my car didn't start right away, so I went back in my apartment. A few minutes later, I tried my car again and it started, so off I went, with no belt. I passed buildings and trees that looked familiar and had a gut feeling something wasn't right. Then I came across a two-car wreck, and I *swear to God* that I had seen the person standing outside the car before in my dream, but that person had been standing over me.

Ken's Second E-mail

Sorry my last e-mail wasn't complete. The alarm started, and I hit send by mistake. Yes, I do think the car had something to do with it. I even go so far as to think that just maybe there was an unseen outside force involved also.

I think the brain stepped in and cause your car not to start
Maybe by subconsciously making you flooded it.
You're brand-new if you left on time you would be in an accident. It was protecting itself. Self-preservation premonition time space memory transfer.

Bill

When I was ten years old, I had a dream. I joined the army and was in boot camp. I was in this long military building, and I was getting my clothes. There were rows of those gold folding chairs that you see in schools or that churches use all the time. I was in the front row, third seat over. There was a platform and some guy measuring us for our pants and shirts. Guess what? Seven or eight years later, I was in Great Lakes, Illinois, at the navy boot camp. I was in the same building, the same seat—everything was identical except that it was the navy, not the army, but even the view outside was the same.

Fred

I dreamed that my friend and his wife were going to have a baby, and when it was time for delivery, they were going to the hospital in a green Volkswagen Bug. They did not own a VW, and she was not pregnant at the time. They called me a few weeks later to inform me that she was pregnant. Several months later, I got a phone call from them telling me how spooky I am. On the way to the hospital, their car broke down. And a green VW Bug stopped and took them to the hospital.

On another occasion, when I was conscious and awake, my wife was washing dishes, and I was standing behind her at the sink. A voice as plain as day said to me, "She's pregnant." No one else in the house—it was just a voice that only I heard. I told her that a voice just told me she was pregnant. A couple of days later, she got a pregnancy test, and it was positive. My name is Fred.

My friends live in Pennsylvania, and I live in Virginia.

Tim's Comments

Fred, your friend was panicking and crying for help. The person in the green VW heard him on a subconscious level. Scientists call this "entanglement" where this frequency/ability takes place.

The cry for help was so powerful that it not only resonated in the present but also in the past. The subconscious was trying to reach out to you to prevent the whole situation from happening is how you saw it. The message came from your friend; he projected it to you. Let him know he is the spooky one!

Fred, if you had understood it to be psychic time travel, you would have known to be there for them at that moment. This is why I feel we should teach this to our children. I believe that anyone has this ability.

So I met a young lady the other day. Her name was Gwen. I enlightened her about my thoughts on time travel. She immediately started telling me about a dream she had about her girlfriend. They were walking down Northern Lights Boulevard in Anchorage, Alaska. It was Saturday night, and they started to argue. Her friend walked into the street and got hit by a car. She was killed.

Gwen's spiraled down into extreme depression, alcohol, and drug use. She said that for the rest of her life, she felt guilty and worthless for causing her friend's death. When she was in her late fifties, she was looking back on her life to try to figure out where it went wrong. She remembered her friend dying and remembered that was where everything had gone downhill for her. Then she woke up. It was all a dream! Or was it?

One week after the dream, she and her friend were walking down Northern Lights Boulevard, and they started to argue. Gwen said she immediately remembered the dream and stopped the argument. She hugged her friend and told her that she loved her. They continued walking down the street when they saw a car zoom by at a high rate of speed only seconds later.

She was able to alter her future by knowing what was about to happen. In the dream, her life had spiraled into such a horrible place over that one event that she was able to send a message back to herself and alter her future/past.

After listening to other people's stories and talking with them, I realized that we all have this ability. We are all psychic time travelers. We are all capable of Space-Time memory transfer

Think of all the wonderful possibilities.

I was talking to a young lady the other night, and I told her about my psychic time-travel project.

She immediately told me about her visions:

For as long as she can remember, she's been dreaming of this young girl of about twelve years old with black hair and very pale, white skin. She finds the girl dead in her dreams, but each time, she is in a different location. She believes it all started when she took a picture of something; there was a shadow of a young girl in the photograph.

Tim's Comments

I cannot think of anything in my theory about a photograph prompting a psychic time-travel event, but if I remove the photo aspect of it, this is what I think.

The young girl has not passed away, yet she is going to die, either by accident or by someone else's hands.

At the moment of her death, she is reaching out for help through entanglement; psychic time-travel also plays a part in it. The young gal is so distressed that she is transmitting her angst through space and time. The people on the same brain wavelength receive the message.

The young gal who told me the story is obviously on the same brainwave frequency and is able to pick up the plea for help.

I told her that she should try to be a time-travel detective. Next time she has that dream, she should try to figure out where it takes place, at what time, and the season. She should find any clues possible and write them down. Every time she has the dream, she should focus on something different. Are the leaves green or brown, or are there no leaves at all? Any clue can start building a case. She must have thought that it was too much to take and that I was weird. I have not heard from her since.

This also means a person can transmit messages back in time to other people. Maybe that is how Nostradamus made all of his predictions and how other people, such as Tesla he was able to see and visualize stuff in their minds and then create it.

So the next five pages are going to be empty. What your assignment is, if you decide to except it, is to write down your own premonitions, déjà vu that have come true.

If you are better at using the computer, you can print it out and make it the size of this book, 6" 9" and paste it in. For some of you this will be a new concept of copy and paste.

Also you can email me a copy and I will put it in my next book, please put déjà vu stories as the subject title, so I can easily identify it.

Your Own Premonitions/ Déjà Vu

Your Own Premonitions/ Déjà Vu

Your Own Premonitions/ Déjà Vu

_____

_____

_____

_____

_____

_____

_____

_____

_____

_____

_____

_____

_____

_____

_____

_____

_____

_____

_____

Your Own Premonitions/ Déjà Vu

Your Own Premonitions/ Déjà Vu

_____

_____

_____

_____

_____

_____

_____

_____

_____

_____

_____

_____

_____

_____

_____

_____

_____

_____

_____

Again, the goal of this book and my YouTube video is to put together a large website where people can go and piece together their story with other like-minded psychic time-traveler detectives.

Let's talk a little bit about the techniques I use to send messages back in time to myself, mainly the lottery and roulette numbers. I am sure this technique will work for anything you are passionate about.

Just before going to bed, I look at the previous winning lottery numbers and repeat them to myself over and over. I visualize the previous morning when I was trying to receive the numbers. The second thing I do is in the morning, when I am just waking and floating in and out of consciousness. I ask myself what the winning numbers are for the lottery and try to visualize myself sending those numbers to me. When I'm drinking my coffee in the morning I sit in front of the chalkboard and the flashing menu board. I study the winning numbers. The reason I do this is to keep up a good routine of studying the winning numbers. When I am in that perfect state of mind and seeing visions through time, I see myself sitting in front of the chalkboard, and the number will be there for me to see.

By memorizing the numbers every night I have also noticed that my memory has improved quite a bit. It used to take me 10 minutes to remember a set of lottery number now after only looking at it two or three times I can remember it. This is very important if you have your vision to be able to remember the lottery numbers after you wake up. It is a good idea to do this every day.

I also practice listening to messages coming in during the day. Sometimes while sitting in my car waiting for Lisa, I relax, close my eyes, and concentrate, trying to visualize the winning lottery number. I also have a pen and paper handy at all times. I will write numbers down that I visualize. However, I will not play the numbers but instead check the accuracy of my visualization. I will also look at the previous winning numbers and repeat them to myself as I am concentrating on a previous time when I know I was listening, such as the previous morning when I was waking up.

So there are two sides to this, like making a phone call. One person has to dial the numbers, while the other person has to pick up the phone. I have to send myself the message, and I also have to be listening for it. The technique is to understand that you are sending yourself messages back in time and that you have the capability of understanding them, which of course is called "enlightenment."

That is one of the main reasons I am writing this book. I feel strongly that if people accept this, they can make changes to their life for the better. Just think—you have a bad feeling about driving somewhere. You decide to stay home; nothing bad happened. You just changed your future by sending yourself a message back in time, and you were able to understand and change your future—space-time memory transfer.

I am not saying stay home from school or work. I am saying wait until you can distinguish a gut feeling from indigestion; until then you should probably continue on with your regular routine.

I mentioned earlier the inspiration I got on the third day. I was to start a website where people can log into different categories, catalog their dreams, and match them with similar dream activity. We will monitor the number of premonitions in a certain category such as airplane crashes, earthquakes, hurricanes, and natural disasters to see if we can determine an algorithm. My hope is that people are seeing these events happening in the future, and they are sending the message through their time line. If we all report our dreams that are disaster related, we could determine, by the number of times a certain dream occurred, the probability of it actually happening. For example, two people saw the twin towers being hit by airplanes in a one-month time frame. The next month, it increased by eight thousand people having the same dream as it got closer to reality.

If everyone relayed what he or she remembered, then by going through all of the information, we could piece together the event. We could probably even identify each person in the event. We could warn them of the upcoming disaster. They would have the opportunity to alter their future. By studying the accuracy of each event, we would be able to prevent such catastrophes by warning all of the website users and in turn, the general public!

Just imagine being able to stop a plane that may crash, or even disappear, from taking off with hundreds of people on it. Or imagine calling a young family and telling them not to go on their driving vacation this weekend so they won't get into an accident. With today's technology, this would not be such a hard website to create. I actually had this particular concept sent to me four times over my lifetime. But now it is a concept that I can envision and see if it comes to life with your help.

I was watching a movie last night in which a couple was on a date for the first time. After the date, the girl turned to the boy and said, "I feel like I've known you forever." The boy said, "Yes, I had that same feeling." I thought about that for a few seconds. When you are going to be with someone for a long time or even a dramatic time, you already know this person. When you meet somebody that you know you're going to spend years with, you are sending yourself messages back in time about the person. This is why you feel that you've known someone for a long time.

Earlier I talked about my girlfriend Melinda. She had a dream about me years before we met. She did not tell me right away; in fact, it took several months before she mentioned it. Melinda and I stayed together for eight years. I, however, have never dreamed of any girlfriends before we met.

2015

So I was on my way to the Yukon River to check on my supplies that the barge company dropped off for me.

There's is a swamp that I need to go across with my four wheeler. Halfway across the swamp I came across a small puppy that jumped out in front of me. It was the cutest little puppy, it was a wolf puppy. It dropped on its front paws, it wag its tail and barked at me in a Puppies bark. I quickly remembered wolves run in packs. I pulled out my shotgun immediately and caulked it.

I looked around.

Looking for the pack of wolves. I looked In front of my four wheeler and the puppy was gone. I could see 100 yards in every direction there was nothing. I figured I may be right over the Wolf den. I did not want to find out. I held the shotgun in one hand and gave the four wheeler throttle and got out of there as fast as I could.

When I pulled up to the landing, there was a family there cleaning up the yard. It turned out to be Charlie White and his family. Charlie is one of the main characters in the reality show *Yukon Men*. I introduced myself. We talked for a while, and he wanted to come out in late September to the gold mine to film my brother and me while we were running our operation. I informed him that I was trying to rebuild an old shaker unit that we had out there. "If I don't get it running, I won't be staying the whole summer," I told him.

He asked me to call him the next day and said that he would talk to his producer and film crew. They wanted to come out that week to see our operation. Maybe I would be on TV sooner rather than later.

So what does this have to do with time travel? I'm not sure, but now I had the opportunity to talk to some people who were doing a reality show, and maybe we could do a small segment about time travel. Then, after I won the lottery, I could branch out from there.

I called Charlie several times, and he was always very glad to hear from me. On July 2, he informed me that the crew was taking off for the holidays and that I should call him after the fourth.

The neighboring camp brought out the investors. They came over and introduced themselves and wanted to borrow a hand auger to do some sampling. After I showed them around my operation, they mentioned that if they could not put a deal together with the neighbors then they would come talk to me. The day passed, and they came back to help me with a small metal building that I was putting together. They also wanted to see my trail to the Yukon River and whether it was passable for them to bring out equipment at that time of the season. I informed them that we had to go over a swamp, and it had been raining for the last three weeks. After putting the metal building together, we headed out for the Yukon at 9:00 p.m. and got there at 11:30 p.m. I loaded up more of the supplies that I had there, and they helped me bring four barrels of fuel off of the beach.

We headed back to camp. I recall looking at my watch. It was 12:30 a.m. We got stuck two or three times but made it across the swamp, up the mountain, and down the mountain. We got back into my camp at 2:45 a.m. It was a long night for sure. They said that they didn't think they could bring equipment across the swamp. They believed it would be too heavy and sink into the abyss.

I told them my brother was flying in the next day. They asked if they could get a ride out of our camp with my cousin. Phil was happy to fly Sammy and Anthony over to Tanana. Thank you for the help, Anthony and Sammy! My brother and I were quite busy finishing up the metal building and making our game plan for the wash plant.

There were a bunch of baby birds nesting in the pipes on the old shaker. We would wait a few more days for them to mature enough to fly away.

I talked to Charlie Wright. He and his film crew had no idea when they would come out. Oh, well. I guess I would have to get on TV my own way.

Another night, I was having trouble sleeping, and I heard some noise outside. I figured it was the black bear again. I looked out, and there was nothing at first, and then a head popped up behind my four-wheeler. But it was not a black bear. It was a grizzly bear—the biggest, baddest bears we have out there. This could have been the one that had destroyed my kitchen twice. I grabbed my shotgun and opened the door. The bear looked up and around. I do not think it saw me. I took aim and pulled the trigger; my gun did not fire. I quickly reloaded it and dropped the bullet that was in the chamber. It fell between my door and steps. I took aim again and pulled the trigger, and this time the gun went off. The grizzly shook its head and ran off. I did not think it was hurt too badly. When my brother got up, we went looking for the bear. There were a few small traces but nothing that we could follow. I did not think I killed the bear, but I think it definitely had a headache for the next several days.

06/14/2011 15:53

The weather out at camp was horrible. I had heard on the radio the other day that we were 300 percent above normal rainfall. I was about to call it quits for the season. We had a swamp we had to go over, which I mentioned earlier, to get our fuel. All of our four-wheelers were having issues. My starter went out in the big four-wheeler 660 that does most of the heavy work. With the swamp not drying out like it normally did this time of year, I just did not want to fight Mother Nature.

I had a lot of time on my hands, and I again watched the movie that I mentioned earlier, *What the Bleep!? Down the Rabbit Hole.* I picked up on several things the last two times I watched it. I mentioned earlier that when I was young, I concentrated and told my mother, without speaking, to come help me. And then the technician had heard me say that the mirrors were not clean. The movie talks about quantum entanglement, in other words, the Einstein-Podolsky-Rosen (EPR) paradox. This theory states that all particles are connected, and what happens to one can happen to another. I believe that my mother and the technician heard me through quantum entanglement. The movie also discusses experiments in which a wired-up person watches photos randomly picked by a computer. Some were neutral photos, and some were photos that would get the subjects upset or aroused. This test was done with hundreds of different people. When people were about to see an upsetting photo, their heart rates would increase. But the brain would also start to show higher activity two or three seconds before the photo even came up. What they believed is that the person was sending that information back in time a few seconds before he or she saw the photo.

August 11, 2015, 11:26 p.m.

I was out at camp, trying to build a wash plant. I had brought my brother out to help me, and he brought his common-law wife, Daisy, with him. She was from Univocal Island. They flew out on July 3. They brought very few supplies with them—a bucket of Kentucky Fried Chicken, a loaf of bread, a dozen eggs, and a few other items. They also brought a gallon of vodka to celebrate the Fourth of July.

On the sixth of July, Neil was ready to start helping me work. We were moving a metal building that came apart in small sections. I had moved everything over to our new location and put the sections together. The building was all together other than putting five hundred nuts and bolts in. Neil helped me for three days straight. When we were finally done, it was a good day.

My brother informed me that he had a few chores to do around our current camp, and he did not want to leave his girl-friend at camp alone because we had bear problems. I had no problem with that, assuming that he would be coming back to work in a few days. He didn't come back until our food supply was running low, and he complained that we needed more groceries. Our camp was in a remote area; everything needed to be shipped or flown in. I had no reason to purchase any more groceries for someone who was just sitting around watching TV and using up my fuel.

I decided not to finish the wash plant. I would probably leave at the end of the month, so I could get back to my time-travel experiments and win the lottery. I finished up the welding on the wash plant when my palm started to itch. I scratched it for about five minutes; it was the palm with the cut on it, and I was thinking of the story my mother used to tell me. Whenever her palm itched, she knew she would be getting some money that day.

I had a feeling something was up. I thought, "This is weird. Something is going to happen today." But I did not think it was going to be money. I went ahead and started to work.

I tried to lift a small sluice box up onto the shaker. It was way too heavy for one person to handle. Frustrated that Neil was not helping me, I thought, "How can I do this by myself?"

I brought the bulldozer around and lifted one half of the box onto the blade of the bulldozer. Then I moved the bulldozer forward, strapped the box to the blade, lifted the blade, and maneuvered the box onto the shaker. I unwrapped the strap that was holding the box to the blade and crawled up onto the blade to maneuver the box into position. I got it right where I wanted it. For some reason, I took a step backward, and I fell off the blade of the bulldozer.

I landed on my back on some metal crossbeams used to hold the blade on. At first, I thought I had broken my back. I started to black out; quickly I took a deep breath and tried to pull myself out from the hole I'd fallen into. I was hurt pretty badly. On my backside, I had a welt as big as an orange, right above my butt. Ow! I was able to keep working and put a good day in even though I was moving quite slowly.

The next morning, I was pretty sore but able to go to work. My brother was not helping me. I e-mailed my pilot, my cousin Phil, and told him I was ready to come home on Thursday, which was three days away. I put in a good day working on the wash plant. That evening, I was building a fire, and I was in an awkward position while loading up the fireplace. The pain hit me and dropped me to my knees. I could barely move for about five minutes. I crawled into bed and was able to cover up and go to sleep with no fire. The next morning, I was in excruciating pain. I could barely get out of bed to go to the bathroom. The pain lasted for about two days. Neil was helping me, bringing me food and filling up my water bottles. He loved me; after all, he was my brother. On the third day, Thursday, I asked Neil if he wanted to come to work with me and help finish fixing the wash plant so we could go gold mining. He said no. He said that he would help me tomorrow. I argued with him a little. He did not know that my cousin was coming out that afternoon to pick me up. I told him that I was going to go to work and that he should check on me at 6:00 p.m.

At 5:00 p.m., I loaded up all of the stuff that I needed to take back to Anchorage. I went to the airstrip and waited for my cousin. He showed up and unloaded the supplies that I had prearranged for him to bring out. I left them for Neil and Daisy. We loaded up all of my stuff, and we were getting ready to leave.

My brother was totally caught off guard. He sped down there with his four-wheeler to ask what was going on and why was I leaving. I told him that I was leaving because I was not getting any help, and I was done for the season.

I got back into Anchorage and was able to relax. I took a hot shower, which helped my back. The next day, I went to the ER to make sure nothing was broken. I had a broken rib—number eleven. Lying there, relaxing, I thought about my hand itching. I did not recognize that as a signal, but now I will.

August 11, 2014

I was back in Anchorage watching a report on TV about the fiftieth anniversary of the big 1964 Good Friday earthquake. I was a year and a half old at that time. I remember that several days before that, on Wednesday, my mom decided to pack up all five kids, and we headed to the airport. I remember that we woke up in Seattle. We went downstairs to a restaurant for some food. There was a newspaper dispenser on the sidewalk, and the headlines screamed, "Big Earthquake in Anchorage, Alaska." The paper explained all the damage the earthquake had done and how everything had been destroyed.

My mom somehow knew that the earthquake was coming and that she needed to do whatever it took to protect her babies, all five of us. I can only imagine what she felt and saw to make her move so fast. She had a sixth sense all her life, just like her mom and her grandmother. She must have seen into the future.

I never thanked her for that, but I'm thinking about her now, and I am thanking her. I hope she can hear me. Thank you, Mom, for being a good mother and protecting us at all costs! Good job, Mom! I love you. I'll see you soon. Rest in peace, Penny Beaton (1925–97).

OK, back to time travel. I was back in Anchorage and starting up my practices again on transmitting thoughts through time. I mentioned earlier that you have to be listening for your thoughts and also be sending your thoughts.

So I was lying in bed, trying to determine which way my thoughts would be traveling when I am receiving a message and when I am sending one. The first thing you need to know is where you are on the planet. Which way is the earth turning, and where are you on it? Where does the sun come up? Visualize the earth rotating and the shadow that the sun makes. Determine exactly which way you are spinning.

The next thing you need to do is to visualize where you were when you sent the message. Try to pick one spot. Routinely use the same area such as a chair, bed, and so on. After you do that, you have to close your eyes and relax and try to think of the spot. Try to listen for a message. Then, when you get to that point in time, you need to sit in the chair and send that message!

For example, let's use a one-hour time frame. Think about where you will be in exactly one hour, and visualize yourself. Try to send yourself a message, and try listening for the message. In one hour, you need to get to that point and try to send that message. It's just like making a phone call in which someone has to dial the phone, and someone has to pick it up at the other end. You will not hear a message unless you send a message and are listening for it. It is very important to remember that.

Again, try different techniques. Remember, we are sending the message from our brain to our brain. We may not need the rotation of the earth or any of that stuff. We are already doing it through déjà vu, premonitions, precognitions, or bad gut feelings. Our brains are already communicating with us back and forth in time; we just need to refine the technique.

Also remember that most people I've been chatting with have dreamed their visions. Maybe concentrate during the day on sending the message to yourself. Visualize yourself while you are asleep.

What works for one may not work for another. Practice all of these, and figure out what works best for you. Also try some good old-fashioned meditation. If you don't know how to meditate, Google it. (I do not know how to meditate. I sit in a hot tub. My sister/editor added that in!) You can check out YouTube or attend a class. Nothing helps you focus as well as meditation. Twenty minutes a day will change your life and help you focus on the vibrations of the universe.

On October 12,1014 I was mainly using time travel to send myself lottery numbers. The window of opportunity is short, so I have to concentrate and practice. I almost get into a sleepy state of mind (almost asleep).

OCTOBER 15, 2014, 8:50 A.M.

I made it back to Virginia. The house was in disarray from the flood that we had had. My wife, Lisa, had to pack everything and store it in my time-travel office. So I was only now getting back into my time-travel practice.

That day, it was announced that a second health-care worker caught the Ebola virus. Wouldn't it have been good if people could send back a warning to themselves not to be where they were when they caught the virus?

Lisa and I filled out cards the night before for the Megabucks lottery. She said that she would get a better picture using her intuition than I would using time travel. This time, after purchasing our tickets, I put them face down in my office. I did not want to look at them until I had enough time to visualize the numbers and try to send them back to myself. I randomly picked a set of numbers. That night, after going to bed, I woke up at three in the morning and checked the lottery number on my phone.

I tried to send the winning numbers back to myself. I visualized myself sitting on the couch with Lisa and tried to send the numbers to my consciousness. After doing this for about an hour and repeating the numbers over and over to myself, I visualized myself looking back at the moment in time when Lisa and I were sitting there. I also visualized going to the room and looking into my consciousness as I was sitting there on the chair, picking numbers.

After doing this several times, I thought, "Why not see if I can put the numbers in Lisa's subconscious?" So I repeated the process but focused on Lisa sitting in the chair filling out the lottery ticket. I concentrated on telling her the numbers.

Lisa got four numbers total. She won the Megabucks number and three of the other numbers; however, it was all on different picks. I mentioned this to her, and she said two of the numbers were the winning numbers. She had a strong sense about them. She only won three dollars.

I looked at my ticket. I got one number right. So at this time, she was better at picking numbers that I was. Ha! Maybe with my new concept of trying to send her the numbers, I would see if I could convince her to be open-minded. I would try sending her the numbers again that night for the new lottery drawing.

Here is one time-travel technique to use if there is a message that you want to send back to yourself—for example, information about a stock that you know such as Yahoo or Apple. You would prepare yourself a quick sentence such as, "Buy Apple at twenty, and sell at one hundred and fifty dollars," or "Let's tell Mom not to take a certain flight, as it will crash."

When you have your message ready to go, say it to yourself every night so you get it down clearly and remember it. The next time you have a déjà vu experience, rather than saying, "Cool. I've seen this before," you yell out your message.

Déjà vu is a common phenomenon, and it may be the most common time-travel door we have. By sending this message back in time, you were altering your past and changing your future.

I'm hoping to teach this to everyone to help prevent accidents and make everyone have a better life.

MAY 18, 2016

I was watching the news, and Flight 804 crashed or was blown up by terrorists. The only survivor at that point was a man who did not board the plane. When he was interviewed, he said he had a very bad feeling in his stomach about the flight. So he decided not to board the plane and took another flight.

This is a clear indication of self-preservation premonition space-time memory transfer.

The Brain was trying to protect itself. We all have this ability.

If he had known about my website, he could have reported his feelings about the plane, and maybe some of the other passengers could have as well. We would have been able to stop the flight and save all those people. The passenger sent himself a message back in time not to board the plane, as evidenced by that horrible feeling in his stomach.

The nervousness you feel inside is called anxiety. Being anxious, I believe, is the feeling that you know something's coming to interrupt your reality, your well-being, and you are sending messages back to yourself in time.

One day, I was watching a movie called *La Bamba*, about singer Ritchie Valens. In the movie, Ritchie keeps having a nightmare in which he goes down in a plane crash and dies. Through most of the movie, he refused to fly because of that recurring dream. At the end of the movie, he and Buddy Holly get into a plane, and it goes down. They all die. Could it have been prevented if he read this book? He was in the prime of his life, sending himself messages back in time, trying to warn himself not to get on the plane. If he had only known about Self-preservation premonition time space memory transfer, he might have prevented his death and changed his future.

Time travel, mind travel, psychic time travel, or space-time memory transfer already exists. We have named this experience premonition, precognition, intuition, and déjà vu. With these psychic phenomena and a few others, I truly believe we are each sending ourselves messages back in time to prevent incidents in our life that are disruptive to our well-being.

I encourage you to go on YouTube and search *premonition* and *precognition*. William Shatner hosts a show that has some interesting thoughts and stories just like the ones I have been telling. The show is called *Weird or What?*, and it's season three, episode seven: "Premonition."

Things to Look for While You Are Having a Dream or a Premonition

- **What time of season is it?** Are you cold? Are people around you wearing jackets or shorts? Where are you? What country? Does everybody look the same?
- **What are your surroundings?** Are you inside or outside? Are you in an airport or an office building? The more details you can remember, the better.

I use my smartphone; I talk in to it in the morning as I'm waking up. It's easy to use the recording app and then put it down on paper when you are awake.

The goal of this book is to enlighten you and to teach our children to be more aware of their ability. I would love to see this in every school, maybe even as part of a required class. Another goal of this book is to help fund the website so people can go and report their psychic time-travel message.

The hope is to prevent or warn about natural disasters, terrorist attacks, plane crashes, train crashes, car crashes, and even murders. The possibilities are endless.

On February/2017

I was proof reading my book cover at the airport. I was on my way to visit Judy in Oregon. When I heard over my shoulder The Psychic Time Traveler.

I turned around and the gentleman said my wife loves those kind of stories.

I told him I was in the final stages of the book and it should be out by the first of the month. He thought that was awesome.

He called his wife over to introduce me to her since she was into that kind of stories.

When she saw the book cover and title she said yes I believe I read that one. She asked my name and I told her. She said yes, you're very popular.

I explained to her that the book has not been published. She had an odd look on her face and said I am pretty sure I read it.

I explained to her how it was possible that she did read it, but in the future, the information was being sent back to her in time.

She took a photo with her camera of the book cover and said she will be the first one to order it.

Now that she met me I'm sure she will be the first one to buy the book, Even though she has already read it in the future.

So the other day I was making copies of the back and front of my Book cover at Staples in Roseburg Oregon. The young lady at the counter took the time to read the introduction of the book. She started asking me questions and I gave her a brief summary. She immediately started to tell me about this feeling that she keeps getting about winning the lottery.

She said she knows she's going to win the lottery. I explained to her that the feeling she is getting is because she actually does win the lottery In the future.

That the brain is filtering the excitement of winning the lottery back through time. Time space memory transfer.

I told her to try my techniques and that would probably help her reach her goal.

Maybe she does not win the lottery until after she reads my book.

To the young lady at Staples I did not want to put your name in the book because when you win the lottery you might have people track you down.

Good luck with your new found ability. Please spread the word.

So scientist believe we only use 10% of our brains power/ability. I wonder what the other 90% of our brain is doing.
     Is it just sitting idle or is it active.
     I personally feel that the other 90% of our brain is active in a big way.
     So active that it only has time to give us 10% of its energy. Space-time energy.
     It makes me wonder is our imagination someone else's reality that our subconscious is visiting.
     The possibilities are growing.
     Did I opened Pandora's Box? If I did it is about time.

From what we know now thanks to the Hubble telescope.
     There are more galaxies then we can count.

In Each galaxy there are more solar systems like ours then we can count.

If the scientists are right about the string theory and quantum mechanics and the plankton scale.

That molecules can be in multiple places at the same time.

That would explain why the other 90% of our brain is not here with us.

I have a feeling we have been thinking small it is time to evolve. Who is with me? Are you ready to evolve to the next level?

When the website is billed I will need a specialized team. Upcoming positions:

Space-time memory transfer analyst. Job description: To read through the incoming premonitions to try to identify a pattern.

Time travel detectives
Description:

Once a Psychic time travel event has been pinpointed, the detective will be at the location at the proper time to try to prevent and change the outcome to a positive outcome.

We will be creating other positions that are involved in running a global time travel security company

My Next Book

I would love to write a book including stories from all kinds of different people and their psychic time-travel experiences. Please e-mail me your story if you would like to be in the next book: timstimezone@gmail.com.

I hope you enjoyed my story. I have also put together a GoFundMe site, so if you want to help support my cause and help me get my website up and running, any donation would be appreciated. My GoFundMe site is under the name Tim Beaton (https://www.gofundme.com/5tmx3cng/donate).

I have also created an online T-shirt store where you can purchase different T-shirts that say "Déjà Vu," "Premonition," "Psychic Time Travel," and other sayings. The sales of the T-shirts will help build and sponsor my website (https://timstimezone.com/).

You can also support me by spreading the word. My Facebook business page is called Tim's Time Zone. Also, if you are an artist or have a good saying for my T-shirts, feel free to contact me. If you can help design the website, that would be great as well.

If you dream of the lottery numbers, don't hesitate to e-mail me and let me know before the lottery draws the number, so I can buy my ticket too. Change one number so you get the jackpot. Send that to as many friends as you can. Five numbers will give your friends one million dollars.

I have some YouTube videos of the gold-mining camp that you can check out. Beaton path mining LLC
https://www.youtube.com/watch?v=3mPlhlQyAYg&t=171s

I put together a T-shirt outlet to help spread the word

To help spread the word I would love the opportunity to do a TV show like the twilight zone but with true stories. I also think it would be nice if shows that are already dealing with the subject matter could fit in a small segment with me and my theory to start spreading the word.

I would be excited and available for any opportunity along those lines

I also could be available for a private consultation or seminars.

Again I would love to see this now concept of time travel in every classroom.

Think of all the life we could save.

I'm trying to think of new ideas on how to generate money for the main website.

I am recently divorced.

So I have been on quite a few dating sites.

I watched a YouTube video on how many people are actually on dating sites now. It turns out to be quite a few. So if you are on a dating site already and you would like to support my idea here is my new dating site. psychictimetravel.net Enter this code to access the website. 9780998719207 I will try to keep it private just for like-minded people like us who have read the book. By using the access code it will keep out spammers and people who are nonbeliever's this site for like-minded people that have had premonitions and believe in the new Space time memory trans-fer theory that I have come up with.

Please help spread the word.

If you ever have had a déjà vu, premonition, precognition or have had that awful feeling in your stomach just before something bad happened, then you have the ability that I have been talking about.

This book is about you.

You are the psychic time traveler. Good luck with your new found ability

Talented individuals that I would like to meet.

Sandra Bullock, Britney Spears, Clint Eastwood, Charlie sheen, Lindsay Lohan
Taylor Swift, The US president to help secure a channel to the White House just in case,
    Those are my top seven but there are hundreds more

I am going to leave the next pages blank with the hope that you will use the rest of this book as a diary/journal for your own psychic time-travel stories. Try to think of a good saying to send back to yourself if you do find yourself in a déjà vu moment. Try to adjust your saying every six months.

Thank you again,
Tim Beaton
January 19, 2017, 2:30 a.m. This is just the beginning

● ● ●

TIM BEATON WAS BORN IN Alaska and is the grandson of the man who discovered the great Iditarod gold strike in 1908. He has moved throughout his life, living in such places as Seattle, Guatemala, and Louisiana, Virginia, though his roots still remain in Alaska.

Since childhood, Beaton has felt a connection to the parapsychological, and his experiences with it inspired him to write *The Psychic Time Traveler.*

Tim D Beaton

_____

_____

_____

_____

_____

_____

_____

_____

_____

_____

_____

_____

_____

_____

_____

_____

_____

_____

_____

_____

_____

_____

_____

_____

_____

_____

_____

_____

_____

_____

_____

_____

_____

_____

_____

_____

_____

_____

_____

_____

_____

_____

_____

_____

_____

_____

_____

_____

_____

_____

_____

_____

_____

_____

_____

_____

_____

_____

_____

_____

_____

_____

_____

_____

_____

_____

_____

_____

_____

_____

_____

Tim D Beaton

Tim D Beaton

_____

_____

_____

_____

_____

_____

_____

_____

_____

_____

_____

_____

_____

_____

_____

_____

_____

_____

_____

_____

_____

_____

Tim D Beaton

Tim D Beaton

Tim D Beaton

_____

_____

_____

_____

_____

_____

_____

_____

_____

_____

_____

_____

_____

_____

_____

_____

_____

_____

_____

_____

_____

_____

_____

Tim D Beaton

_____

_____

_____

_____

_____

_____

_____

_____

_____

_____

_____

_____

_____

_____

_____

_____

_____

_____

_____

_____

_____

_____

_____

Tim D Beaton

_____

_____

_____

_____

_____

_____

_____

_____

_____

_____

_____

_____

_____

_____

_____

_____

_____

_____

_____

_____

_____

Tim D Beaton

Tim D Beaton

Tim D Beaton

Tim D Beaton

_____

_____

_____

_____

_____

_____

_____

_____

_____

_____

_____

_____

_____

_____

_____

_____

_____

_____

_____

_____

_____

Tim D Beaton

Tim D Beaton

Tim D Beaton

162

Tim D Beaton

Tim D Beaton

Tim D Beaton

_____

_____

_____

_____

_____

_____

_____

_____

_____

_____

_____

_____

_____

_____

_____

_____

_____

_____

_____

_____

_____

_____

Tim D Beaton

Tim D Beaton

Made in the USA
Middletown, DE
06 May 2017